The Boys' Brigade in Plymouth 1887–1983

William J. F. Lapthorn

Sir William Alexander Smith, 1854–1914, founder of The Boys' Brigade. This is the most popular picture of the Founder and used in this centenary year as the front of the membership card.

This version of the book is virtually as originally published, presenting the work of William JF Lapthorn. There are now additional pages at the back providing information about the publisher, Arthur L Clamp.

The republishing project is being managed by Arthur's grandson, Steven Gibson. We aim to find all the research that he was involved in publishing, preserving it for the next generation as part of 'The Clamp Collection'.

INTRODUCTION

William Alexander Smith was an officer in the 1st Lanarkshire Rifle Volunteers and a Sunday School teacher at the Woodside Mission, Glasgow. He and the other teachers were struggling to retain the senior boys in the school who felt they were too old for such a thing and he feared that those who left were unprovided for at a critical age. The boys who did remain were often compelled to attend unwillingly by their parents and so became uninterested, unruly and difficult.

It was suggested to William Smith that he might bring his military experience to bear on this problem and so was conceived the idea of bringing boys together with discipline and banding them together with *esprit de corps*, and on the 4th October, 1883, a Company of thirty Boys was formed and called *THE BOYS' BRIGADE*.

This novel idea soon spread over Scotland, not without opposition, however, by those who thought it too military, and south of the border into England. On 22nd June, 1887, the 1st Plymouth Company was formed at Sherwell Congregational Church under the Captaincy of Leonard E. Stoneman with five officers, four N.C.O.'s and fifty-two boys.

The idea flourished in the Three Towns, as our city was then, and the 2nd, 3rd, 4th, 5th and 6th Companies were formed in 1888, the 7th and 8th in 1889 and the 9th in 1890. The 1st, 2nd and 3rd Stonehouse Companies in 1890, 1892 and 1895 respectively, the 1st Devonport in 1892 and the 2nd and 3rd Devonport in 1895. Subsequently the Plymouth, Stonehouse and Devonport Battalion was created on the 4th July, 1895. Stonehouse and Devonport were deleted from the title on 12th April, 1915.

One of the highlights of the programme in the late 1890's and early 1900's was the annual camp when Companies joined together and those who were able to attend, usually about 100, enjoyed the experience of travelling to such far off places as Thurlestone and Downderry. In 1912, at the invitation of the Cork Companies, eighty officers and Boys from Plymouth embarked on the S.S. *Kenmare Castle* at Millbay Docks for the journey to Roche's Point, County Cork, Ireland, where a combined camp was held. In August, 1914, when the war started most of the officers in Camp were called to the forces leaving few beyond the rank of staff-sergeant to carry on.

During the war the work in the Companies continued, sometimes with difficulty because of a shortage of Officers, but certainly with patriotic fervour. The 4th Company dropped football and substituted rifle drill and shooting for older Boys at the Plymouth Gas Company's range. The band assisted at recruiting evenings organised by the Citizens Recruiting Committee and led parades of the Plymouth Citizens Defence Force. Many enlisted in the forces and as early as November, 1914, seventy-six members and ex-members of the 4th Company were already serving. Other Companies also provided many men and inevitably many did not return.

After the war there was an upsurge in recruitment so much so that Companies had to institute "waiting lists" because the premises available could not accommodate the numbers wishing to join.

Jubilee year in 1933 was celebrated world wide and a great International Camp was held at Dechmont, Kirkhill, near Glasgow, at which there was a contingent from the Plymouth Battalion. To celebrate the Silver Jubilee of King George V in 1935 loyal messages were borne by teams of runners from all parts of the country to London. The Southern Message, with which the Plymouth Battalion was directly concerned, travelled 412 miles from Penzance to London. Plymouth Companies were allocated the route from Truro to Plymouth.

The 1939–45 war with black-out restrictions, air raids and evacuation was an extremely difficult period but Companies carried on as best they could with many Boys doing duty with Civil Defence for which they were awarded a special badge. Again many officers had to leave to join the forces. After the war again there was an increasing interest in the Movement, more Companies were formed in parts of the city that were entirely new to the B.B.

The Festival of Britain in 1951 was recognised by messages of loyal greetings being brought by runners from all parts of the British Isles to Buckingham Palace.

1954 was the Founder's Centenary and representatives of the Plymouth Battalion attended the International Camp held on the playing fields of Eton College. A Battalion Display was held at the Royal Citadel. 1958 was the 75th Anniversary and Plymouth was represented at the Royal Review at Balmoral.

To-day there are 16 Companies in the city operating in Anglican, Baptist, Methodist and United Reformed Churches. Besides the normal activities of badge classes many hundreds of pounds have been raised by means of sponsored events, flag days, house to house collections, etc. for charities such as the R.N.L.I., Guide Dogs for the Blind, Seamen's Mission, handicapped children, the aged, etc. as well as taking part in these efforts the Junior Sections have also collected a great deal of money for the work of the various denominational missionary societies.

The Battalion is fortunate to have P. M. Bindschedler, LL.B., F.I.L., as President in this Centenary Year and indeed to have been served in this office by such men as L. Bond Spear, P. R. Harvey, W. S. Adams, W. R. Stibbs, W. D. Hoskyn, J. P. Robb, W. J. Keast and the late Earl of Mount Edgcumbe. Tribute must also be paid to the officers, both male and female, who week by week give unstintingly of their time, talents and energy to the work of their Companies. Over nearly 100 years thousands of Boys have benefited from their leadership and have become Christian men and good members of society.

The Plymouth Battalion is marking the Centenary with this publication in which some of the events over the years are recorded and which it is hoped is a reflection of the OBJECT OF THE BOYS' BRIGADE:

The Advancement of Christ's Kingdom among Boys, and the promotion of habits of Obedience, Reverence, Discipline, Self-Respect and all that tends towards a true Christian Manliness.

We are indeed grateful to the *Western Evening Herald*, Arthur L. Clamp, David White, Editor, *B.B. Gazette*, Miss Muriel Ellis, Brigade Archivist, H.Q. London, and the many members, ex-members and interested friends who have so kindly loaned photographs, books, written accounts, etc.

If any Company or special occasion has been omitted please accept our apologies. The size of this title has restricted the volume of information given and the selection of photographs from the numbers available.

As a personal memento of the Centenary, every Boy in the Plymouth Battalion was presented with a copy of this publication and a Bible donated by the Trinitarian Bible Society, on Centenary Day, Tuesday 4th October, 1983, in the Plymouth Central Hall, Saltash Street, Plymouth.

William J. F. Lapthorn,
34 Sherford Crescent,
Elburton,
Plymouth,
PL9 8DU
October, 1983

Arthur L. Clamp,
203 Elburton Road,
Plymstock,
Plymouth,
PL9 8HX
October, 1983

The Plymouth Battalion, 1983

1st Plymouth Company Salisbury Road Baptist Church.
2nd Plymouth Company St. Andrew's Church
3rd Plymouth Company Crownhill Methodist Church
4th Plymouth Company St. Jude's Church
5th Plymouth Company Plymouth East Methodist Church
6th Plymouth Company Hope Baptist Church
7th Plymouth Company Peverell Park Methodist Church
8th Plymouth Company Ford Baptist Church
9th Plymouth Company Methodist Central Hall, Plymouth
11th Plymouth Company Zion Methodist Church
14th Plymouth Company Derriford United Reformed Church
16th Plymouth Company St. Edward's Church
17th Plymouth Company Christ Church
18th Plymouth Company Pilgrim United Reformed Church
1st Plympton Company St. Mary's Church
2nd Plympton Company Ridgeway Methodist Church

The original record of the Plymouth Battalion held at Brigade Headquarters, Glasgow, showing the change in office bearers and companies during the period 1888 to 1891.

LEONARD E. STONEMAN,
Captain, 1st Plymouth Company.

MR. STONEMAN first heard of The Boys' Brigade in the spring of 1887. For some three or four years a Sunday Evening Service for Boys had been held at the Sunday School (Sherwell) with which he is connected, but the order at this meeting was not all that could be desired, and The Boys' Brigade promised to supply the necessary weapon for keeping the Boys interested and under control. With the consent of the Church Officers, the 1st Plymouth Company was formed, with these Boys as a nucleus. It was enrolled in June, 1887, with Mr. Stoneman as Captain. From that time onward the Company has increased its hold on its Boys and its influence for good. It was decided that the Sunday Evening Service should be continued, but along Boys' Brigade lines, and the wisdom of this step has been amply proved. The hearty singing, reverent demeanour in prayer, careful attention to the address, and orderly dismissal, make it a model Boys' Meeting. The doings of the 1st Plymouth attracted the attention of other schools, so that in April, 1889, the Plymouth Battalion was formed. Mr. Stoneman was appointed Secretary, and still retains that post. The Battalion has met with varying success; but in order to put the work on a firmer basis, the Council, in October last, came to the conclusion that nothing would be more likely to be useful than a Battalion Head-Quarters. A full account of the working of this scheme was furnished in the last number of the *Gazette*, suffice it to say that Mr. Stoneman's special charge is the Lantern Service for Boys on Sunday evenings from 8-15 to 9-15, which has proved a great success, and has an average attendance of about 200 Boys.

Sgt. George Hellyer

This picture of Sgt. George Hellyer of the 3rd Plymouth Company (Courtney Street Congregational) was taken in 1893. Both his son Wilf, and the grandson Roy, were officers in the 1st Plymouth Company (Salisbury Road Baptist). Roy is now President of the Newcastle-upon-Tyne Battalion and a co-opted member of the Brigade Executive. Another grandson Malcolm Harrison, is a lieutenant in the 1st Plymouth Company, and a great-grandson Christian Harrison, **aged nine years,** is a member of the Junior Section.

PLYMOUTH.

A CHURCH PARADE was held on Easter Sunday evening, when five Companies were represented. Mr. Reginald Bewes, President of the Battalion, took the chair, and an address was given by Mr. E. F. Anthony.

THE Volunteer Drill Hall and grounds having been placed at the disposal of the Battalion, a full day's work was arranged for Easter Monday. In the morning two football matches were played: 1st Plymouth First Eleven *versus* 4th Plymouth, after a hotly contested game, resulted in a victory for the former by two goals to nil. The other match—1st Plymouth Second Eleven *v.* 9th Plymouth—was also won by the 1st Company's team, the goals being three to one.

IN the afternoon the Battalion paraded in the Guildhall Square, where they were joined by a detachment of the 1st Torpoint Company, and marched to Millbay, headed by the 1st Plymouth Company Brass Band. The Battalion having been formed into line, awaited the arrival of Lieut.-Colonel G. A. Heseltine, R.M.L.I., who had kindly consented to inspect the Boys. He was received with the general salute. Having dismounted, Colonel Heseltine carefully inspected the lines.

THE Drill Competition for the Colours then took place. The competing Companies were the 1st, 3rd, and 9th. "In awarding the Colours to the 9th Company," wrote the Inspecting Officer, "I did not in any way wish to disparage the efforts of the then holders (1st Company), but as I understood the 1st Company had held them for the year, I thought that as No. 9 drilled equally well with No. 1, it was but fair that they should hold them now, as an additional inducement to attention and *esprit de corps*."

B.B. Gazette, June, 1891

PLYMOUTH, STONEHOUSE, AND DEVONPORT.

It has been a great pleasure to the Officers of this Battalion to receive a visit from Mr. W. A. Smith, Brigade Secretary. On Wednesday, 27th January, he inspected the 1st and 2nd Stonehouse, the 3rd Plymouth (the members of which presented him with an address of welcome) and the 1st and 6th Plymouth Companies, and at each of the three parades he expressed himself as very much pleased with the turn-out and steadiness of the Boys. On Thursday morning he went on board H.M.S. *Renown* and also one of the torpedo-boat destroyers, H.M.S. *Rocket*, lunching afterwards on H.M.S. *Indus*. In the evening he met the Officers of the Battalion at a social gathering at the house of the Battalion President, in the course of which he delivered a most earnest and impressive address, which will long be remembered by those who heard it; family prayers brought this very enjoyable evening to a close. On Friday he went to Exeter and met the Officers of the Exeter District Committee, and on Saturday morning left Plymouth for London. Officers in the West of England feel very grateful to Mr. Smith for sparing time to come to see them.

1897

The Boys' Brigade Gazette

In the late 1880s and early 1890s there were few Battalions in existence and accounts of their activities were able to be published in the *Gazette*, and Plymouth Companies featured regularly. With the growth of the movement throughout the land and the limited space available these very informative articles had to be discontinued.

Boys' Brigade Heroes.

BRAVE DEED OF A 1st PLYMOUTH BOY.

ON September 1st, 1890, the steamer *Eleanor* was chartered by the congregation of Hope Chapel, Plymouth (with which the 10th Plymouth Company is connected), for a trip up the river Tamar. This river divides Devonshire from Cornwall and flows into the Plymouth Sound, and being very picturesque and navigable for some twenty-five miles, is a favourite excursion for those "on pleasure bent." Shortly after arriving at Calstock, a boy named Alfred Deacon, five years of age, fell from the paddle-box of the steamer into the river, and was swiftly carried away by the strongly-flowing tide. A lad named Henry Renton, without divesting himself of his clothing, and without a moment's hesitation, plunged into the river, and reaching the little fellow, kept him afloat until they were both rescued by the ferry boatman and another. Renton was at the time sixteen years of age, and a member of the Brass Band of the 1st Plymouth Company of The Boys' Brigade. In order to defray the damage done to his clothing and watch (a prize won at the swimming matches) a sum of money was collected from onlookers and handed to him. His comrades in the 1st Plymouth, to show their appreciation of his gallant act, subscribed for an Oxford Bible, which was presented to him at the Company Flower Show by Captain Stoneman, and which he holds in his hand in the picture. A few days later the Mayor of Plymouth presented Renton with the silver medal and framed certificate of the Port of Plymouth Humane Society.

The 3rd and 9th Plymouth Companies have had a very successful winter session. The Reading and Games Rooms have been opened every night and were highly appreciated, whilst the Bible-class Young Christians' Meeting, and Company Service have all been largely attended. A special feature has been the monthly "Route March," headed by the Company's Drum and Fife Band. These marches are very popular with the Boys. The Handbell ringers (under Lieut. Pearse) are in constant request for entertainments, etc. The Annual Outing of the 3rd, 9th, and 10th Companies is fixed for Whit-Monday, and will this year, by the kindly co-operation of the Officers of the 1st Torpoint Company, take place at Torpoint. A very large muster is anticipated. The Company mustered strongly at the "Annual Inspection" on Easter Monday. A special summer programme is in preparation for the Companies, who meet all the year round. Present strength, 80.

The 10th Plymouth Company, connected with Hope Chapel U.M.F.C., continues to make satisfactory progress. It is now twelve months since we started, having then the use of the schoolroom only one night a week. Now we can boast of having two nights, and in addition a Company Bible-class on Sunday mornings. During the winter months we have had coffee suppers given by the Officers and friends. On one occasion, after an entertainment by the Boys, the ladies of the church were so highly pleased with them in their drill that they decided to give them a supper the following week. We have on the roll between thirty and forty Officers and Boys. A monthly squad attendance competition causes a deal of interest. On Whit-Monday we intend joining the 3rd Company in their annual Company Outing at Torpoint.

1892

PRIVATE HENRY RENTON,
1ST PLYMOUTH COMPANY, BOYS' BRIGADE,
AND THE BOY THAT HE SAVED FROM DROWNING.

4th Plymouth Company (St. Jude's)

This Company photograph was taken on Boxing Day, 1905, at Seven Trees and, together with a report on the work of the Company, (page 8) appeared in the B.B. Gazette.

THE BOYS' BRIGADE

PATRON:
H.R.H. THE PRINCE OF WALES, K.G.

VICE-PATRON:
HIS GRACE THE ARCHBISHOP OF CANTERBURY.

THE PLYMOUTH, STONEHOUSE AND DEVONPORT BATTALION.

SESSION 1901-1902.

Plymouth:
ADLARD BROTHERS, OCTAGON WORKS.

DETAILS OF COMPANIES.

Company.	Connected with	Officers.	Rank.	No. of Boys.
1st Plymouth	Sherwell Congregational Church	Mr. E. F. Anthony Mr. C. R. Serpell Mr. S. E. Bowden Mr. B. Chaffey	Capt. Lieut. ,, ,,	75
3rd Plymouth	Courtenay Street Congregational Church	Mr. J. S. Wright Rev. J. T. Maxwell Mr. H. R. Pearse Mr. J. H. Stanlake Mr. W. J. Davey Mr. S. E. Cotton	Capt. Chaplain Lieut. ,, ,, ,,	194
5th Plymouth	Emmanuel Church	Mr. W. F. Clatworthy Rev. G. Scholey Mr. A. Anderson, Junr.	Capt. Chaplain Lieut.	25
6th Plymouth	Charles' Church	Mr. A. L. Lewin Mr. A. H. Bowden Mr. R. C. Pitts Mr. A. E. Grant	Capt. Lieut. ,, ,,	66
1st Sto'house	St. George's Church	Mr. A. J. Milton Mr. A. E. Spender Mr. F. Dunaway Mr. T. S. Crocker Mr. J. W. Bradford Mr. C. F. Hill	Capt. Lieut. ,, ,, ,, ,,	50

Total of Battalion—Officers, 23; Boys, 410

NEW COMPANIES.

2nd Plymouth.   Connected with St. Andrew's Church.
4th Plymouth.   ,,   St. Jude's Church.
5th Plymouth (attached). ,,   St. Augustine's Church.
1st Torpoint.   ,,   St. James's Church, Torpoint.

Jubilee Number.

The Camp Rook AND "Caw"-sand News.

Hatched Daily at the Boys' Brigade Camp, Cawsand.

Not registered for transmission abroad. | JUNE 1900. | [Priceless.

Editor's Notes.

The Editor wishes to record his thanks to Mr. Prior for the loan of a very useful and compact typewriter, which very materially adds to the appearance of the "Rook" and which has been the means of bringing it to its present state of perfection and up-to-dated-ness. This is only one instance of Mr. Prior's many kindnesses we might quote.

The Camp is very fortunate in having such an expert typist as Mr. R. C. Pitts, to whom a large amount of the success of the paper is due. No doubt the near neighbours of the printing office would like it removed a little nearer—Cawsand, but the popular demand for good literature is so great that even sleep must give way before its advancing overwhelming flood.

Camp  Notes.

The CANTEEN will be open each day from 9 a.m. till 5 p.m.

Stone Pop, Sweets, Chocolates, &c., of the finest quality, at moderate charges.

Terms: Strictly Cash.

No Cheques or Paper Money taken.

Misfortunes never come single,
And so, like birds of feather,
The marriages and the deaths
Are printed close together.

LEONARD & CO.,
Chemists, &c.,
CHAWSAND.

Camphor Pills a speciality.

Toilet Powders, Rouges, etc.

Use
Moonlight Soap

WORTH A GUINEA A BOX.

The original and best for puddings frying, and cooking. The most nourishing for Infants, Invalids, and everybody.

One 6d. square will make a pint and a half of strong nutritious soup.

Ask your Grocer for it, and see that you get it.

The Camp Rook

The leading page of the camp news published every day. Besides camp activities news of the Boer War was reported and it is said that the good people of Cawsand often relied on the "Rook" for such information. Sometimes a B.B. officer would go to the village square and proclaim the news for all to hear. County cricket scores were also a feature.

Membership Card

This card was issued to Private William Stibbs, aged 13 years, who in later years became Captain of the 4th Plymouth Company.

Battalion Camp, Downderry, 1904

The lads shown are believed to be S/Sgts. getting hot water from the boiler. The cold water carrier can be seen on the left. The stiff collars and waistcoats, complete with watch chains and medallions, could not have been very comfortable "camp gear".

Representative Companies.
The 4th Plymouth Company.

WE are pleased to publish this month a photograph of the 4th Plymouth Company which will attract attention to the work of the Brigade in the South-West of England. This Company was started in 1902 by Mr. Edward V. F. Shaw, in connection with St. Jude's Church and it soon became firmly established. Unfortunately, at the end of 1903 Mr. Shaw left Plymouth and for a year no one could be found to undertake the captaincy, though by means of an occasional meeting the Boys were kept in touch with, and the Company not allowed to lapse. In January, 1905, a new Captain was found in Mr. John H. Stanlake, and at the first drill 22 Boys were present. By the close of the session the roll had increased to 60, and the Company had come to be looked on as one of the most vigorous in the town. That its membership has in no way fallen off in the present session is shown by the accompanying photograph, which was taken at a Boxing Day gathering.

Of course the re-organization has not been all plain sailing, for the Company Headquarters are situated in a poor part of the town, and great difficulties have been met with in providing adequate accommodation. This has now been overcome by the acquirement of a vacant carpenter's shop which a fatigue squad converted into comfortable Headquarters, which are open every night for reading, games, and gymnastic classes, whilst the other agencies employed in Company work, viz. :— Band, Savings Bank (in connection with the Post Office Savings Bank), athletics, football, etc., are in full operation.

A high standard of discipline is rigorously enforced, to which everything is subservient. Mr. Stanlake has had several years' experience as an Officer in the now defunct 3rd Plymouth Company, and associated with him in the work is Mr. Pearse, also an Officer of experience, who has served from a boy in the 3rd Plymouth since its inception—a period of 17 years.

The Company is a unit of the Plymouth, Stonehouse, and Devonport Battalion, which has been in existence for 10 years, though isolated Companies have been at work in the Three Towns for nearly twice that length of time. Numerically, the Battalion is one of the smallest in the country, for it has had to face many difficulties in the past which few other towns experience. A great difficulty is that the Three Towns form one of the most important naval and garrison centres in the Kingdom. Hence drill, uniform, etc., are no novelty to the Boys who are accustomed to seeing such every day of their lives, and many of them also have elder brothers or parents in one of the Services, who have a good-natured contempt for the Brigade. Further many of our older Boys enter some branch of the Services, and just when they are forming a good back-bone to a Company they leave it. To these difficulties must be added a constantly shifting population which causes many changes in all ranks of a Company, and also the financial difficulty which seems to weigh heavily.

Despite it all, however, the Battalion has done good work in its ten years of existence. It makes a prominent feature of swimming with the result that a very large percentage of the Boys are good swimmers. Two of its members have received the Brigade Cross for Heroism, gained by saving lives from drowning. The Battalion Summer Camp is also a popular and successful feature of the year's work, whilst a football competition carried out under league rules is always keenly fought out. Occasional united Drills and Church Parades are held which are well attended, and serve as a reminder to the Boys of the wider organization to which they belong.

THE BOYS' BRIGADE.

4TH PLYMOUTH COMPANY.
Connected with St. Jude's Church.

RULES.

1.—Members must be Boys between 12 and 17 years of age.

2.—Every Member must be a total abstainer, and is strictly forbidden to smoke.

3.—Members must at all times set an example of good conduct to their Comrades and other Boys, and conduct themselves in a quiet and orderly manner, when going to and from Parade, Church, or other Meeting.

4.—Members must come on Parade in Uniform, sharp to time, looking smart and clean.

5.—Members must give prompt and cheerful obedience to all the orders of their Officers and Non-Commissioned Officers.

6.—Members must always salute their Officers when they meet them, or go up to address them, either on or off parade, and will always use "Sir," when addressing an Officer. Boys in Uniform will salute Officers of other Companies in Uniform.

7. During Drill there must be strict attention, and no talking in the ranks except when "standing easy." In Church there must be quietness and attention, and perfect reverence throughout the Service.

8.—Any member who misses two consecutive Meetings (Drill or Church), without good and satisfactory reason, is liable to be struck off the Roll.

9.—Any Member changing his address will at once intimate the change, *in writing*, to the Captain of the Company.

10. Members will be held responsible for making themselves acquainted with these Rules and with all the Orders posted on the Company Notice Board, and for giving attention to all intimations made at Drill or Bible Class.

These Rules will be strictly enforced.

The Officers Expect every Boy

To read every day the portion of Scripture laid down in the Boys' Brigade Scripture Union Card, and to remember his prayers morning and evening.

Never to use bad language.

Always to prefer DUTY to either pleasure or inclination.

Always to endeavour to maintain the purity, kindliness, courtesy, and mutual confidence that should prevail in a Company of The Boys' Brigade.

At all times and in all places to maintain the honour of the "4th PLYMOUTH," and to remember that the credit of the Boys' Brigade is in the keeping of every individual Member of the Company.

Remember, Boys, your Officers wish to be your *friends*. Be frank and open with them, and do not hesitate to come to them if ever you are in trouble or difficulty

JOHN H. STANLAKE, *Captain*,
STADDON VIEW,
SALISBURY ROAD, PLYMOUTH.

Company Rules

These rules were first printed in 1907 and are probably identical to the originals of 1902. In the main they still apply to-day.

6th Plymouth Company (Charles Church) 1919 – 20

Members of the Company pictured outside the church are wearing the uniform of The Boys' Brigade Cadet Corps, being part of the Devon Territorial Forces Association to which Companies were allowed to belong with permission of their respective churches. The Brigade withdrew as a whole from the scheme in 1924. The Sergeant seated in the 3rd row (4th from left) is Roy Boon and the Army Officer (left of centre) was Capt. H. A. Brown who, while at Crownhill Convalescent Home, assisted the Company especially in physical training. He later became the secretary of Notts Cricket Club.

Plymouth Guildhall, 1919

Plymouth Guildhall was on Wednesday the scene of the twelfth annual inspection and demonstration of the 4th Plymouth Company (St. Jude's) Boys' Brigade. There were 64 boys on parade, and a large number of friends were present. The vicar (Rev. J. W. Sturdy) presided, and the inspecting officer was Lieut.-Colonel F. H. Neish, commanding the 1st Battalion Gordon Highlanders, who was accompanied by Capt. and Adjutant Bell. The officers of the company are:— President and chaplain, Rev. J. W. Sturdy; Captain J. H. Stanlake, Lieutenants R. H. Pearse, W. H. Callicott, F. Prowse, H. S. Woodward, J. H. Waller, F. Simmons, and G. H. Start.

After the inspection there was a parade and march past under the command of ex-Lieut. E. W. Higginson. The band (Bandmaster, Mr. A. Lee) played during the inspection, and a company of buglers gave a series of bugle calls. A display of company drill was followed by the presentation of certificates and badges. These included the King's Badge, which is given under certain stringent conditions, and is only to be worn on occasions according to regulation. The boys, who received the King's medal at the hands of Colonel Neish, were Sergt. S. Skelly, Sergt. R. Polmear, and Corpl. W. Tonkin. This is the first time the King's medal has been awarded in Plymouth. Ambulance certificates were awarded as follows:—1st course, Corpl. Adams, Lance-Corpl. F. Bray Privates Henry Gillard, Edwin Pledge, Charles Barnes, Thos. Roberts, Will Jolley, Sam Callicott, E. Honeychurch, Will Denning, Henry Locke, and William Challacombe; 2nd course, Privates Jewell, Martin, and Hawkins. Sergeants' stars (for drill efficiency) were awarded to Colour-Sergt. Hayward, Sergt. Lush, and Sergt. Polmear.

Colonel Neish said he found the accoutrements and the instruments of the band very good. There was steadiness on parade, though some of the boys were looking about, and the general appearance was very good indeed. He always noticed that if boys had a little drill and a little discipline it improved their personal appearance. (Applause.) The march past also was very good, as was the playing of the band, while the buglers were excellent. He did not know who their instructor was, but he congratulated him. (Applause.) He was much struck with the smartness of their action and the clearness of their notes. (Applause.)—The Vicar tendered hearty thanks to Col. Neish, and said the Boys Brigade was an excellent adjunct to the work of the Church. He appealed for financial help towards the boys' camp in the summer at Mothecombe.

4th Plymouth Company (St. Judes) 1920 – 21

The gymnastic squad of the Company, pictured outside the church, looking very businesslike in their gym gear. J. H. Stanlake and H. R. Pearce are the officers in uniform with the Rev. W. A. Weekes standing. J. H. Waller (centre) was the instructor. He was succeeded by Tom Chapman (left centre) who with Ernie Taylor (right centre) still live in the city.

Fatigue Squad, 1927

4th Plymouth Co. "spud bashers" in action under the watchful eye of the camp cook.

Greetings

The "inside" of the greetings card sent to each boy in the reserves of the 4th Plymouth Co. (St. Jude's).

> ### The Boy Reserves.
> The Training Reserve of The Boys' Brigade.
>
>
>
> ### The Officers and Staff send Christmas Greetings and Best Wishes for Happy Days in 1924.
>
> Just do your best,
> And leave the rest
> To Him who gave you Life, —
> And Zeal for Labour, —
> And the Joy of Strife, —
> And Zest of Love, —
> And all that lifts your soul above
> The lower things.
>
> John Oxenham.

Happy Days

The five smiling faces seen at the Rennie Point camp in 1926 belong to Percy King, Albert Easton, Ed Smith and Jimmy Robinson with Ernie Withell in front, all members of the 2nd Plymouth Co. (St. Andrew's).

Bathing Party

Members of the 4th Plymouth Co. showing off the latest in 1926 swim wear! The summer house, used by the Mildmay family, will be recognised by visitors to Mothecombe beach.

Arrival at Camp, 1924

This was the formal parade by the 4th Plymouth Co. immediately upon arrival at Mothecombe following a march from Yealmpton Station with colours flying and kit completed with water bottles loaned by the Royal Marines. The band is playing and the Officers are saluting as the Camp Flag is raised. The 4th first camped at Mothecombe, in 1907 and except for a break of two years have camped there each year since.

2nd Plymouth Company, 1925

Although the Brigade withdrew from the Cadet Corps scheme in 1924 the St. Andrew's Company is still wearing the uniform. This picture was taken in the Guildhall Square after attending parade service at the church and shows the trophies won during the session. Percy Harvey, the Company Captain for many years, is seated in the centre.

Camp Officers, 1925

The officers of the 4th Plymouth Co. (St. Jude's) camp dressed in full uniform for an "official" photograph. The old style caps and badges can be more clearly seen in this picture. Back row, left to right: W. Stibbs, Dr. Cheyne Wilson (an X-ray specialist) who was always the camp doctor, S. Blagdon, E. Hawkins, H. R. Pearce, Rev. W. A. Weekes and J. H. Stanlake.

Day Trip, 1924

Members of the 4th Plymouth Boy Reserves enjoying their refreshments on a day visit to the Company camp at Mothecombe. In naval tradition they are wearing the white cap covers for summer.

Wembury Camp, 1928

The 4th Plymouth Co. in camp at New Barton Farm, Wembury, ready to move off on church parade. This was one of the two years that the Company did not use Mothecombe and it is reported that the site was rather exposed to the elements and not very comfortable.

Church Parade, 1928

The 4th Plymouth Co., seen again in formation beside St. Jude's Church, waiting to receive their membership cards from the Company chaplain Rev. W. A. Weekes. The Life Boys are in line on the right wearing winter dress caps, i.e. without the white cap covers.

Mothecombe Camp, 1927

Members of "C" tent, 4th Plymouth Co. await inspection by the Duty Officer. The tent commander is Sgt. T. Harvey, with L/Cpl. T. Farrant and Privates Cox, Petherbridge, Cornish, Newman and Wilson. The squad looks rather pensive, perhaps wondering if the blankets have the correct number of folds or maybe the D.O. is already inside the tent with eagle eye scanning the floor for that elusive blade of grass.

The Silver Jubilee Run, 1935

The Southern section of the Loyal Message to King George V travelled 412 miles from Land's End (Penzance) to the Royal Albert Hall, London. Plymouth Companies carried the message from Truro to Plymouth and here we see the bearer, Staff Sgt. G. F. Buckler (2nd Plymouth Co., St. Andrew's), with escorts Col. Sgt. A. J. Tickell (3rd Plymouth Co., St. Augustine's) and Sgt. C. Pettitt (11th Plymouth Co., Stonehouse Methodist Mission) handing on to the Exeter and District runners in the Guildhall Square on Friday 26th April.

Junior Football Team, 4th Plymouth Co.

The players pictured outside St. Jude's Church in 1933 with the Rev. McMaking, Lt. Bowden and S/Sgt. Saunter are Knox, Pike, Rowe, Kneebone, Saunter, Millman, Strong, Vicary, Harvey, Clemo and Pease.

Flash back to the Twenties

Here we see Lord Mildmay inspecting the 4th Plymouth Company after morning service at Holbeton Church. After walking the ranks it was his custom to address the Company, usually to compliment them on their "turn-out".

2nd Plymouth Company, 1939

This picture taken by St. Andrew's Church and shows Captain Percy Harvey backed by a strong Company. The gentleman in the black homburg hat is the Rev. Whitfield Dawkes and, on his right, is Bill Howard who finished his term as President of the West of England District in April of this year (1983). Seated third from the right is Ron Sanders who served the Company for many years eventually becoming Captain.

N.C.O.'s Certificate

Awarded to Boys who have passed the necessary written examinations and who are thought to have the character and power of leadership.

Annual Treat, 1930's

The people of Holbeton, dressed in their Sunday best, enjoy the annual treat of watching the 4th Plymouth Co., led by Drum Major S/Sgt. Stanley Willcocks, march through the village on the way back to camp after being inspected by Lord Mildmay. On one occasion Admiral Sir Deric Holland Martin, Second Sea Lord, who was staying at Mothecombe House, was asked to do the honours, and in order to be suitably clad he borrowed a hunting bowler hat from Mrs. Helen Mildmay-White and an umbrella from Dame Lucille Sayers. The Company was later instructed to discontinue wearing the Cadet Corps uniform.

Ambulance Certificate

This certificate was awarded to Private Kenneth Stibbs, who, during the Second World War while serving in the Royal Air Force, was killed in a raid over Holland.

THE BOYS' BRIGADE.
1ST PLYMOUTH COMPANY'S VISIT TO NORTH CORNWALL TONIGHT.

1938

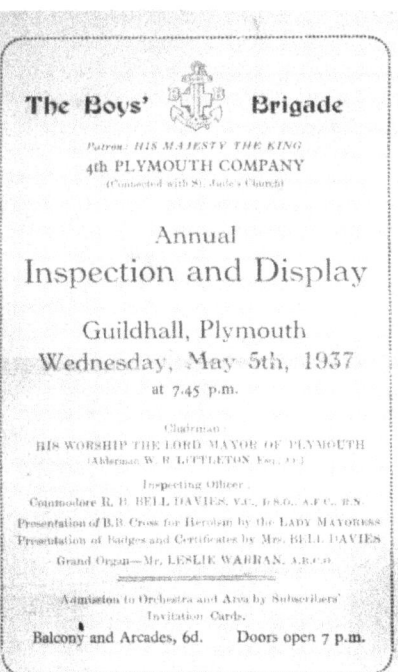

During their camp eighteen months ago a group of boys of the 1st Hastings Company, in the course of a walk, unaccompanied by an officer, dropped into the parish church at Guestling. They saw there a notice about the proposed installation of electric light in the church. Admiring the church and "feeling good," they made a collection on the spot, and left their contribution behind them in a duly inscribed envelope.

The incident had long since been forgotten when the rector of Guestling wrote saying that although the Church Council, shortly before the boys' act, had decided to drop the electric light project, the boys' example had so inspired the congregation that they revived the scheme, which had now been carried to a successful issue. The 2s. grew to £44, the new lighting has been installed, and the boys who had inspired the effort were invited to the service, at which the light was switched on.

FOR WORLD PEACE.

Sunday, February 6, is Boys' Brigade League of Nations Sunday, and should be so observed in every company Bibleclass. While we may sometimes feel dissatisfied and disappointed with the small measure of practical success which the League seeks to attain, the ultimate triumph will depend on the witness of Christian peoples everywhere, and it is our duty and privilege so to train our boys that they will play their part in bringing about that world peace which can only come through the influence of Christ's Kingdom. And the extension of that Kingdom is the primary purpose of The Boys' Brigade

VISIT TO DELABOLE.

Tonight the 1st Plymouth Company (Clare Congregational Mission) is going over by 'bus to pay a visit to the 1st Delabole Company to give a demonstration programme of B.B. activities.

This is being done on the invitation of the captain (Rev. J. W. Walker), a Methodist padre who is responsible for the formation of 3 or 4 new companies in North Cornwall. He is very keen on extension, as everyone ought to be when they have a good cause to "extend."

The Brigade secretary, Mr. Geo. Stanley Smith, M.C., O.B.E., paid Mr. Walker a special visit from London two months ago to accompany him on a tour of inspection of the new companies which he (the latter) had fostered and fathered and paid a very fine tribute to the untiring enthusiasm of Mr. Walker and the very excellent results of his pioneer work.

We hope that shortly the 1st Delabole Company will be able to pay us a return visit and stay some week-end in Plymouth.

Mothecombe Rescue

During this annual display of the 4th Plymouth Company Percy Kneebone was presented with the B.B. Cross for heroism for saving life while in camp at Mothecombe in 1936.

After Church

The 5th Plymouth Company (St. Mary's Church, Cattedown) pose for a company photograph after attending Church parade on the 26th February, 1939. The Company Captain, A. J. B. Lamb, is seen with the Rev. C. H. Garland, Lieut. G. A. Rowe and W/O Fennell.

6th Plymouth Company, 1947

The first picture of the Company taken on the green beside Hope Baptist Church, now the site of the Church hall. The officers are from left to right: Howard Pike, Lieut., Rev. Chas. Dyer, Chaplain, William J. Keast, Capt. and Ernest Glover, Lieut. later Captain of the 7th Plymouth Company (Peverell Park Methodist). Six of the lads shown, Brian Keast, Derek Pomeroy, Roy Tamlin, Brian Thomas, Ron Walters and David Pendock eventually became officers serving with the 6th Plymouth and 7th Plymouth Companies and the 1st Tavistock.

8th Plymouth Company 1948

In this picture taking during the Company camp at South Hooe, Bere Alston, Mrs. Betty Collins and Mrs. W. Hutchings, two stalwart supporters of the Company are seen seated in the front. Among the boys with Lieut. Derek Collins are P. Brown, T. Williams, C. Simpson, G. Bowden, C. Ryder, S. Cox, and K. Trewartha.

Bukit Ruma, 1944

After the house **Bukit Ruma** at Newton Ferrers, Devon, was requisitioned by the R.A.F. it was re-named *Battenway*. The 5th Plymouth Company were given permission to camp there and among the group taken in the grounds are Mrs Edna Chapman (seated extreme left) and Eric Chapman (seated fourth from left) with Ernie Prinn, "Boyso" Rendle, Ralph Williams, Peter Coleman, Harold Williams, Roy Rowe, Arthur Brooking and Ron Luckes.

Annual Inspection, 1949

Programme cover showing the tower of St. Andrew's Church. The Inspecting Officer, J. P. W. Hingston, M.B.E., is an "Old Boy" of the Plymouth Battalion.

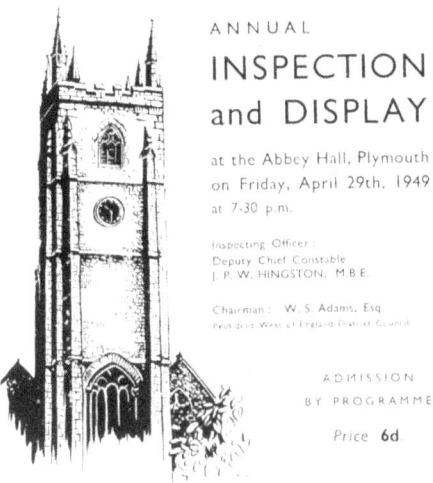

Memorial Gifts, 1947

This tent and six bugles were presented to the 4th Plymouth Company by the Old Boys' Association as a memorial to those members and ex-members who lost their lives in the 1939–1945 war. Sgt. I. Manley and his squad stand outside ready for inspection.

5th Plymouth Company, 1946

Identified in this picture of the Company band, taken in the Astor Field, are S. Leat, R. Rowe, J. Stapleton, C. Searle, H. Williams, D. Newman, M. Rich, G. Harley, R. Boyes and R. Abbott.

Off to Denmark, 1947

Sgt. Harold Williams, 5th Plymouth Company (Embankment Road Methodist) waving farewell as he left North Road Station to attend the International Rally in Denmark as one of the two Westcountry representatives of the Brigade. Harold is now a lieutenant in the 9th Plymouth Company (Plymouth Central Hall).

Briar Hill Farm, 1945

Roy Rowe, Sid Warren and Trevor Druce are among the rear party of the 5th Plymouth Company (Embankment Road Methodist) camp at Newton Ferrers, enjoying breakfast before facing the task of clearing the site.

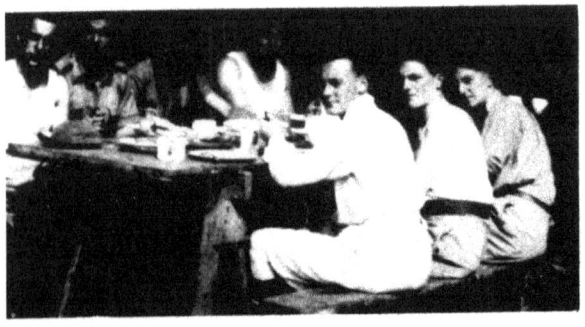

5th Plymouth Company, 1945

This picture of the Company was taken behind Embankment Road Methodist Church in the Astor Playing Field which had just been vacated as a barrage balloon unit site. The two officers in the centre are E. R. Chapman and A. J. B. Lamb both Captains during their service with the Company.

Victory Parade, 1945

With the Drum Majors saluting the Lord Mayor and Lady Mayoress, Lord and Lady Astor, the combined bands of the 4th and 5th Plymouth Companies lead the B.B. contingent on what is now the Royal Parade. The ruins of St. Andrew's Church can be seen on the right.

THE BOYS' BRIGADE
PLYMOUTH BATTALION

VISIT OF THE BRIGADE SECRETARY
G. STANLEY SMITH, Esq. O.B.E., M.C.
Swarthmore Hall, Mutley Plain, Plymouth
THURSDAY, 17th MARCH, 1949

Toast List

To Propose — To Reply

The King
W. R. STIBBS, Esq.
President, Plymouth Battalion

The City of Plymouth
T. THORNTON WILLS, Esq. — Ald. H. J. PERRY, J.P.
Vice-President, Bristol Battalion, — Lord Mayor of Plymouth
West of England Representative
on Brigade Executive.

The Boys' Brigade
ANDREW SCOTLAND, — G. STANLEY SMITH,
Esq., M.A., PH.D. — Esq., O.B.E., M.C.
Director of Education, Hon. — Brigade Secretary
Sec. Plymouth Youth Committee.

Visit of the Brigade Secretary

The toast list on the occasion of the visit of the Founder's son.

Chaplain's Example

The Chaplain of the 9th Plymouth Company (Methodist Central Hall), the Rev. Clifford O. Ladlow, putting on a brave show and perhaps giving an example that cleanliness is next to Godliness.

THIS IS TO CERTIFY

that Pte David C Bennett
of the 4th Plymouth Company
has attended the First Year Course in
Ambulance and First Aid to the Injured
and has passed a satisfactory Examination

Signature of Lecturer
Signature of Examiner
Signature of Captain or
Battalion Ambulance Convener
Date April 28th 1947.

First Aid

This certificate was awarded to Private David Bennett of the 4th Plymouth Company (St. Jude's) for proficiency in elementary ambulance and first aid. David is at present the Captain of the Company.

9th Plymouth Company

These lads pictured at camp sometime in the late 1940's are not wearing sun hats as their predecessors did many years before but small baths or washing bowls. The lad on the extreme right is Raymond Pedlar, J.P., now Battalion Extension and Consolidation Officer.

Ladies Night

In appreciation of their loyal support during the year the ladies are entertained. Those who have long served the Plymouth Battalion will recognise many faces at this gathering in the late 1950s.

Battalion Review, 1954

The Reviewing Officer, Air Vice-Marshal T. C. Trail, C.B., O.B.E., D.F.C., presents the Battalion Colours to the 5th Plymouth Company. Colour Party. S/Sgt. R. Ledden, Lieut. P. Coleman, Cpl. D. Tuthill, Lieut. H. Williams and S/Sgt. E. Williams.

Festival of Britain, 1951

The team of runners from the 6th Plymouth Company, Derek Pomeroy, Brian Thomas and Terry Norman, before setting off the carry the "Message to the King" on the next 4½ miles stage from Ivybridge to the Bittaford viaduct. W. J. Keast, Company Captain, is seen on the left.

Battalion Church Parade, 1954

Lieut. E. Chapman, Lieut. H. Williams, W/O F. Hodges, S/Sgt. E. Williams, and S/Sgt. R. Ledden of the 5th Plymouth Company provide the Colour Party as the Battalion enters the Plymouth Central Hall from Saltash Street. Captain R. Gregory follows leading the Company.

 The Boys' Brigade PHYSICAL TRAINING

P.T. Certificate

Awarded to boys who had attained the necessary standard in all physical training activities. This certificate had to be obtained before qualifying for the P.T. Badge.

W.O.E. District Football, 1949

In the final of the Football Shield against the Bristol Battalion at the Eastville ground Dave Burley (6th Plymouth) could not stop this one going in and Alfie Eastlick (6th Plymouth), with mouth open wide, cannot believe it. Plymouth eventually won by 2 goals to 1.

8th Plymouth Company, 1950's

The Life Boys are pictured outside Ford Baptist Church with their leaders, Marjorie Hutchings, Florrie Wilson and Jean Tucker.

Founder's Centenary Camp, 1954

Two thousand Boys from every corner of the world camped together on the playing fields of Eton College to celebrate the birth of the founder. In typical English "summer" weather the mud and rain did not deter the campers and even the advance party remained cheerful when a "Burma Road" had to be constructed with 1,500 railway sleepers to enable the lorries to enter the site. The Plymouth contingent pictured, B. Chapman (5th) C. Farrell (9th), L. McEwen (4th), P. Whitfield (7th), W. S. Adams (Batt. Pres), E. Lukes (7th), R. Pomeroy (6th), A. Keast (1st), E. R. Chapman (District Field Officer), B. Tonkin (5th), R. Gartrell (9th), J. Underwood (2nd), and P. Brown (6th).

Tableau, 1950

Members of the 1st Plymouth Co. (Salisbury Road, Baptist) form a tableau with their instructor Bert Andrews during a gymnastic display.

Founder's Centenary, 1954

The front cover of the programme for the display to celebrate the birth of the founder. The performance was of a very high standard and much appreciated by the many hundred spectators who were present.

Helston Farm Camp, 1950

The Company Colour covering the piled drums of the 8th Plymouth Co. (Ford Baptist) surmounted by the Cross makes the focal point for the Drumhead Service in the camp field.

The Astor Football Cup, 1951 – 52

The first winners of this "knock-out" competition were the 6th Plymouth Co. (Hope Baptist). Back. D. Pomeroy, D. Cooper, P. Brown, T. Norman, C. Gill and J. Crowley. Front: M. Parnell, M. Bowden, W. Lapthorn (Lieut.), A. Davies, W. J. Keast (Company Captain), R. Pomeroy and G. Fyfe.

The Plymouth Programme

ON WEDNESDAY the Plymouth Battalion celebrates the anniversary by holding a display in the Citadel, when the Lord Mayor of Plymouth (Ald. E. W. Perry) and the Commander-in-Chief, Plymouth Command (Adml. Sir Alexander C. G. Madden), have accepted invitations to attend.

The guard of honour for the occasion will be formed by the 5th Plymouth (Embankment-road Methodist) Company, winners of the battalion squad drill competition.

Events will be:
Demonstration of squad drill by 5th Plymouth.
Massed bands by 1st Plymouth (Salisbury-road Baptist), 4th Plymouth (St. Jude's Church), and 5th Plymouth Companies.
P.T. display by 2nd Plymouth (St. Andrew's Church) and 6th Plymouth (Hope Baptist) Companies.
"Treatment and Transportation"—showing the practical uses to which the Wayfaring and Ambulance Badges can be put—by 6th Plymouth and 7th Plymouth (Peverell Park Methodist) Companies.
Parallel bars and tableau by 4th Plymouth.
"Where there's a wheel there's a way"—cycle maze item—by 1st Plymouth.
March of the toy soldiers by 9th Plymouth (Methodist Central Hall).
Competition relay games by 1st, 3rd (Whitleigh Methodist), 8th (Ford Baptist), and 12th (St. Budeaux Baptist) Companies.
"The Boys' Brigade salutes the founder" by 1st and 5th Plymouth Companies.

Church Lads Brigade, 1958

Prior to the Executive meeting, the President welcomed an Officer and four Boys of the Church Lads Brigade who were staying in Plymouth for a few days before attending an International Camp. These CLB members came from Barbados and were being entertained by Mr Witham (Captain) and Parents and Friends of the 14th Plymouth Company (Mutley Baptist).

Company Choir, 1958

The intense concentration of the 5th Plymouth Company (Embankment Road Methodist) choir as they strive to reach that top note during their item at the West of England District Display held in the Town Hall, Torquay.

Company Awards

St/Sgt. A. Davies congratulates members of the 6th Plymouth Company (Hope Baptist) on winning Company trophies. Pte. C. Brock, First Aid Cup, Pte. M. Fleet, P. T. Cup and Pte. G. Fyfe holding the Squad Shield.

The First Step

This certificate was awarded to David Bennett in 1951, the first step on the ladder to his present position as Captain of the 4th Plymouth Company.

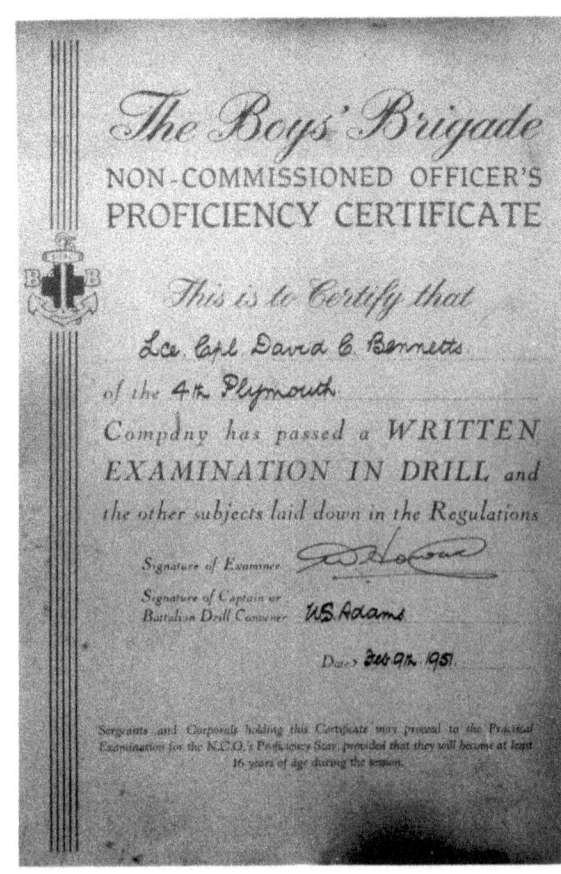

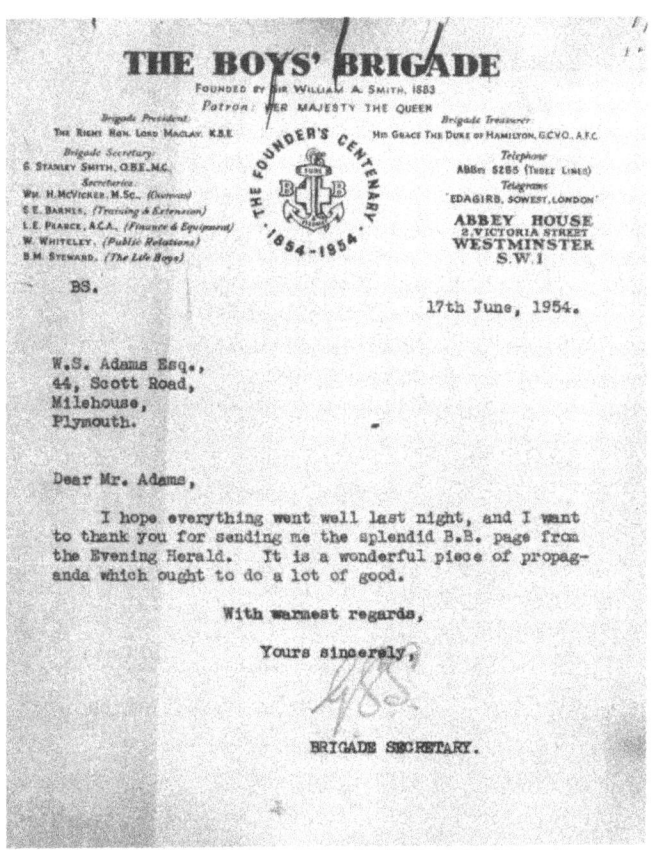

Founder's Son Letter
The letter received from the Brigade Secretary, G. Stanley Smith, O.B.E., M.C., son of the Founder, on the occasion of the Battalion Display at the Citadel to celebrate the centenary of the birth of William A. Smith.

Battalion Review, 1958
Held on Plymouth Hoe, the Battalion Review was for many years a feature of the annual programme when Senior Service officers were invited to attend. On this occasion the Reviewing Officer was Group Captain A. W. B. Barrett, R.A.F., and is seen, accompanied by the Battalion President, W. J. Keast, meeting winners of the Queen's Badge. Sgt. W. Clark, 2nd Plymouth Company (St. Andrew's), Sgt. T. Hughes, 8th Plymouth Company (Ford Baptist), Sgt. C. Drinkwater and Cpl. C. Hookway both of the 7th Plymouth Company (Peverell Park Methodist).

Civic Parade 1956
With the clock in St. Andrew's Church tower showing 12.30 p.m. the colour party provided by the 5th Plymouth Company, Arthur Rugg, Eric Williams, Brian Chapman, Colin Petley and Roy Ledden, march past the Lord Mayor, Mr. Edwin Broad, who takes the salute by the flagstaff in Royal Parade. The Battalion President, W. J. Keast, and the Battalion Secretary, W. S. Adams, are also present.

Cross for Heroism
Previous winners of the cross

1904	Pte. J. Hocking	2nd Plymouth Company
	Pte. P. Hocking	2nd Plymouth Company
1906	Pte. J. Minhinett	2nd Plymouth Company
1936	Cpl. P. Kneebone	4th Plymouth Company
1937	Pte. C. Wickett	2nd Plymouth Company

The Fearless Five of the 5th

Obviously pleased that their heroic deed had been so recognised Cpl. Raymond Willis, Cpl. Raymond Bailey, S/Sgt. Alan Dore, Cpl. Christopher Robson and Sgt. Peter Maxwell are seen after their awards.

NEWS FROM THE BOYS' BRIGADE

PUBLIC RELATIONS SECRETARY- W WHITELEY. ABBey 5265
ABBEY HOUSE, 2, VICTORIA STREET, LONDON S.W.1.

18th September, 1963.

B.B. AWARDS TO PLYMOUTH BOYS FOR RESCUING FOUR PEOPLE

The Boys' Brigade Cross for Heroism has been awarded to Alan Dore and The Boys' Brigade Diploma for Gallant Conduct awarded to Raymond Bailey, Peter Maxwell, Christopher Robson, and Raymond Willis, all of the 5th Plymouth (Embankment Road Methodist Church) Company.

The Boys were camping in Cornwall and on 29th July 1963 while swimming at Maenporth Beach near Falmouth, one of the Officers saw two boys in difficulty in the large breakers. A whistle blast alerted the B.B. Boys and Alan Dore (17 years) after swimming about 100 yards reached the younger of the two boys. Against a fast out-going current Alan, with the assistance of Christopher Robson (15 years) brought the boy to the beach. The boy's older companion was helped ashore by Raymond Bailey (15 years).

About ten minutes later a woman was seen being carried out by the current, with her husband trying in vain to reach her. Raymond Willis (15 years) and Christopher Robson dived in and reached the woman, but with the heavy waves were having a difficult time. Alan Dore, followed by Peter Maxwell (16 years) and Raymond Bailey also swam out to give much needed assistance. Between them the Boys brought both the man and the woman safely to the shore. Non-swimmers had to wade in and assist at the last stage as the Boys were completely worn out by their efforts.

But for the prompt action of these Boys and the fine swimming by Alan Dore, the four persons would have been swept out to sea.

: : : : : : : : : : : :

NOTE - The Captain of the Company is:-
Mr. K.J. Banfield, 15, Channel View Terrace, Lipson, Plymouth.

Abbey House,
Westminster, S.W.1.
39/63.

Queen's Men

Lt. Col. H. F. C. Kimpton, R.M., accompanied by the Battalion President, W. J. Keast, congratulating winners of the Queen's Badge. From the right: P. Harber (7th Plymouth), P. Brown and R. Pomeroy (6th Plymouth), R. Ledden and E. Williams (5th Plymouth) and L. McEwen (4th Plymouth). The seventh remains unidentified.

Eyes to the Front
At the Founder's Centenary Display in 1954 the Guard of Honour, provided by the 5th Plymouth Company, (Embankment Road Methodist) stands rigidly at attention with eyes straight ahead as the Commander-in-Chief, Plymouth Command, Admiral Sir Alexander C. G. Madden, carries out the inspection on his arrival at the parade ground of the Royal Citadel. Among the Guard A. Rugg, D. Carter, P. Coleman, R. Trewin, C. Petley and C. Pengelly can be identified.

Official Invitation
The invitation sent to those who were to occupy the VIP enclosure at the Review. The Battalion has been very fortunate over the years in having the support of many high ranking officers of all three Services.

THE BOYS' BRIGADE
Founded by Sir William A. Smith, 1883
Patron: H.M. THE QUEEN
PLYMOUTH BATTALION

The President and Officers request the pleasure of your company at the Battalion Review on Plymouth Hoe Friday, June 2nd, 1961, at 8 p.m.

Reviewing Officer: Group Capt. D. E. HAWKINS, D.F.C., R.A.F.
Accompanied by the Deputy Lord Mayor & Rev. R. L. Ackroyd, M.A.
(President, Plymouth Free Church Council)

Ticket holders must be seated by 7.40 p.m.

Physical Training, 1960 – 61
During this period the squad of the 6th Plymouth Company gave many displays at carnivals, fetes, etc. at various places in Devon and Cornwall and are here posing before performing at Gunnislake. Back left to right. B. Harries, A. Crisp, M. Jolly, E. Reburn, D. Greygoose, R. Scoble, P. Cornish and D. Brown. Front left to right: J. Jeffrey, P. Cotter, R. Hatherley, T. Fallon, J. Eascott, D. Fallon, P. Dann and G. Millett.

All Aboard

The day spent aboard this ship was exciting, competitive, entertaining and very tiring but thoroughly enjoyed by the "crew" and "passengers" alike. The items including Work Ship, P. T., King Neptune and the "Crossing the Line" ceremony, Sea Shanties, Deck Games, and the Ship's Band were all of a nautical flavour.

THE LIFE BOYS
PLYMOUTH AREA

A Day on board the Training Ship
"Life Boy"

THE SHIP WILL BE BERTHED AT
SALISBURY ROAD BAPTIST CHURCH HALL
on
SATURDAY, MARCH 11th, 1961

You are invited to be on board not later than 2.15 p.m.

VISITING OFFICER
THE LORD MAYOR OF PLYMOUTH
Alderman F. J. Stott

CHAPLAIN . Rev. L. MERRETT

Ships Orders 1/- each, which will permit bearer to board . . .

THE BOYS' BRIGADE
FOUNDED 1883
Patron: HER MAJESTY THE QUEEN

5th Plymouth Company
EMBANKMENT ROAD METHODIST CHURCH

21st Annual
INSPECTION & DISPLAY
IN THE DIAMOND JUBILEE YEAR OF OUR CHURCH

The Embankment Road Methodist Hall, Plymouth
WEDNESDAY, 30th APRIL, 1958, at 7.30 p.m.
Doors open at 7 p.m.   (Please be in your seat by 7.20 p.m.)

Chairman:
THE LORD MAYOR OF PLYMOUTH
(Alderman L. F. PAUL)
Hon. Vice-President, Plymouth Battalion

Inspecting Officer:
A. J. MOXEY, Esq.
Captain, 5th Exeter Company
(St. Thomas Methodist Church)

PROGRAMME: ONE SHILLING   DOOR B

Proficiency Competition, 1961

At the twenty-fifth anniversary on 30th November of the 5th Plymouth Company, the President (W. S. Adams) presented the Battalion Colours to the company as winners of the competition.

Royal Visit, 1961

Members of the 5th Plymouth Company hand-bell team showing the Duke of Edinburgh how well they can "ring the changes" during his visit to the city in connection with the D.O.E. Award Scheme. Pictured in the grounds of Devonport High School for Boys are K. J. Banfield, Company Capt. D. Brown (6th), W. Carter, G. Pellow, D. Richardson, T. Hall, D. Bishop, G. Stoneman, R. Tate and P. Maxwell.

Display
Pictured on the front of the programme are Dave Summers, 1st Plym., Chris Robson, 5th Plym., Bruce Tindell, 9th Plym. and Raymond Bailey, 5th Plym. receiving their Duke of Edinburgh Gold Awards.

The Boon Trophy
The Boon Trophy, presented to the most proficient Company during the Session, is being received on behalf of the 5th Plymouth Company by Sgt. Raymond Willis. Raymond achieved one hundred per cent attendance at Parade Night and Bible Class over a period of five years. Pictured also Raymond Bray, Brigade Vice-President (ex-Captain 1st Plymouth Co.), K. J. Banfield, J.P., Company Captain R. H. P. Boon, donor of the trophy, Rev. W. J. E. Tregenna-Piggott, O.B.E., R.N.Retd., Chaplain, and W. S. Adams, Battalion President.

THE BOYS' BRIGADE
PLYMOUTH BATTALION

Now a Captain
Stephen Congdon who served through the ranks of the 6th Plymouth Co. receiving the Queen's Badge from the Battalion President (W. J. Keast). Stephen is now Captain of the newest Company, the 16th Plymouth (St. Edward's, Eggbuckland).

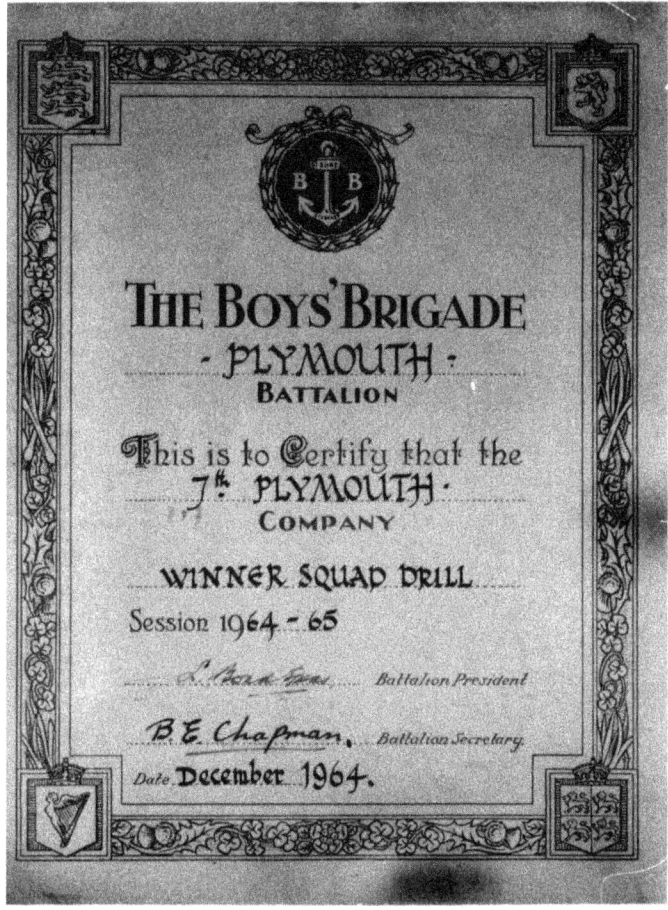

Civic Parade, 1966

The colour party, Capt. Don Reeby, S/Sgt. D. Glasson, G. Williams, R. Dean and G. Howe, of the 7th Plymouth Company march past the Lord Mayor, Mr. Percy Pascoe, after attending the Methodist Central Hall. Also at the saluting base are the Rev. John Ashplant, Chaplain, 9th Plymouth Company (Plymouth Central Hall), Mr. L. Bond Spear, Battalion President and Eric Chapman, District Field Officer.

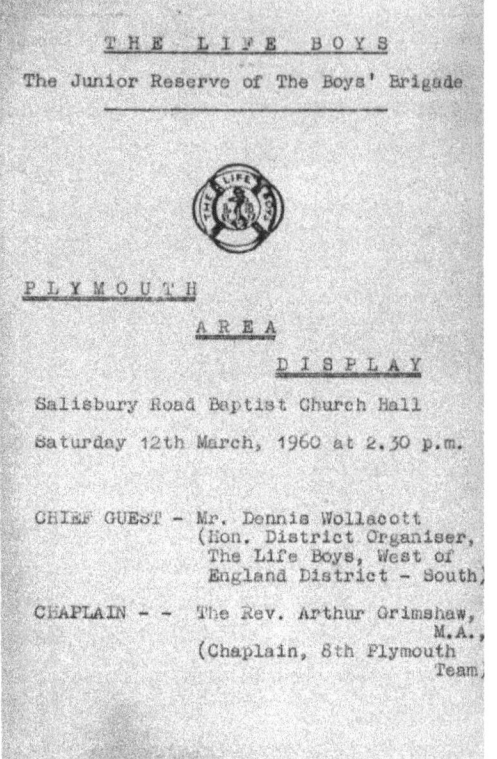

Don't Forget!

Boys of the 5th Plymouth Company getting last minute instructions from Company Captain Ken Banfield for the "novelty" item during their Annual Display in 1961.

All Smiles

Cpl. David Brown (Duke of Edinburgh Bronze Award), Sgt. Roger Matthews (Queen's Badge) and Cpl. Michael Holland (Duke of Edinburgh Bronze Award) at the Annual Inspection of the 6th Plymouth Co. (Hope Baptist), in 1960.

Church Parade, 1977

The band of the 1st Plymouth Co. (Salisbury Road Baptist) leading to the Company and the Girls' Brigade to church.

W.O.E. District Band Competition, 1979

This competition attracted bands from all parts of the District and was held on a perfect June day which showed the Hoe and the city at its best and provided a spectacle to be remembered.

7th Plymouth Co., 1977 Band Call

Members of the 7th Plymouth Co. (Peverell Park Methodist) band waiting to take part in the West of England District Band Competition at Weston-super-Mare in 1977. The drummers are A. Day, G. Drummond, P. Blundon and the buglers D. Bultitude, R. Stone, R. Burley, M. Brown and A. Gould.

Cross Country Runners, 1976

Simon Westlake, Ian Cox, Stephen Brown, Michael Campion and Jonothan Nicholle, members of the 6th Plymouth Co. (Hope Baptist) Junior team, before the start of the West of England District race.

Civic Parade, 1976

The Lord Mayor, Mr. Ivor Thompson, and the Battalion President, the Earl of Mount Edgcumbe, have a word with the Junior Section of the 1st Plympton Company (St. Mary's), after morning service at George Street Baptist Church. Pictured also are the Rev. Duff Stephenson, who conducted the service, Battalion Vice-President Tom Babb, the Countess of Mount Edgcumbe and the Lady Mayoress.

On the Water Front

In this photograph, taken in the late 1970's, we see the Battalion band, with band officer Richard Congdon, giving a display on the Barbican during Sutton Habour Regatta Week. In the background is the Mayflower Memorial with the "Stars and Stripes" and "Union Flag" flying, to the right the tower of Mount Batten. In recent years the Battalion band has been in great demand and has taken part in many of the events taking place in the area.

Anchors Boys

The officer-in-charge, Mrs Yvonne Heale, waits as the Deputy Lord Mayor, Mr. Denis Dicker, chats with the Anchor Boys during the Annual Inspection of the 5th Plymouth Company (Embankment Road Methodist).

Juniors on Parade, 1976
The column sweeps round the corner as the band of the 8th Plymouth Company leads the Junior Sections of the Battalion to their Annual Service held in that year at Ford Baptist Church.

An Achievement
These smiling faces in 1980 are happy to show their Duke of Edinburgh Gold Awards achieved at last. The four in uniform are Paul Capstack, Dypak Mistry, Paul Colwill and Gareth Parnell all members of the 5th Plymouth Company (Embankment Road Methodist).

Battalion Colours
Battalion Vice-President and Training Officer Jim Stapleton, presenting the Battalion Colours to members of the 6th Plymouth Company (Hope Baptist) after the Company had won the squad drill competition in 1974. Acting as colour party are Philip Tregidgo, Colin Tregidgo, David Saunders, John Knight and Stephen Charlton, while Company Captain Raymond Pomeroy looks on.

Anchor Boys, 1982

Martin Seager, Andrew Round, Thomas Harris, Lee Pearce, Martin Wills, Murray Quest, and Dominic Walsh, Anchor Boys in the 2nd Plympton Company (Ridgeway Methodist), concentrate on the job in hand during their meeting.

Help to Others, 1980

Members of the 6th Plymouth Company (Hope Baptist) give toys and books, purchased with money raised at their Annual Inspection, to the Children's Ward at the Royal Naval Hospital, Stonehouse.

Guide Dogs 1980

The Lord Mayor of Plymouth, Mr. Graham Jinks, an Honorary Vice-President, waves aloft a cheque for £460 for the Guide Dogs for the Blind raised by a sponsored walk by the Battalion. Some of the lads who took part are seen in the Lord Mayor's parlour where the presentation took place.

Visit to Exmouth, 1981
Anthony Pierce, Stephen Vaughan, Mark Cockrell, Darren Lamble, Jason Gilbert, Russell Smyth, Mark Tustian, Mark Roskelly, Neil Stephens, Andrew Jones, Darren Oddy, Matthew Rawlings and Andrew Townsend of the 18th Plymouth Company (Pilgrim United Reformed Church) pictured during their camp at Exmouth.

Missionary Rally, 1982
At Christmas time each year the Junior Sections collect money for their own denominational missionary societies. At this annual rally representatives are presenting tokens for the amounts collected to Miss Talbot who has served with the Baptist Missionary Society in Nepal.

Waking up Peverell, 1982
After a lapse of some years the reformed band of the 6th Plymouth Company arouses the neighbourhood as the Company parades to Hope Baptist Church.

16th Plymouth Company, 1982

The newest Company in the Battalion pictured outside St. Edward's Church, Eggbuckland, proudly showing off their new uniforms before setting out to attend their first Battalion Church parade. The Company Captain, Stephen Congdon, is assisted by two lady officers Kay Congdon and Janet Paterson.

Centenary Party, 1983

Waiting in eager anticipation of demolishing the cake are Robert Skinner, Darren Langley, Neil Hatherley, Paul Eveleigh, John Alden and Stephen Gribble at the 6th Plymouth Company Junior Section Centenary party.

The Christmas Spirit, 1981

Members of the 6th Plymouth (Hope Baptist) and 16th Plymouth (St. Edward's Eggbuckland) Companies join forces to tour the area singing carols to raise money for Cumberland House, Devonport, a home for mentally handicapped adults.

Civic Parade, 1983

The Lord Mayor, Mr. Reg Scott, accompanied by the Battalion President, Mr. Peter Bindschedler, LL.B., F.I.L. and the Rev. Graham Sharpe, takes the salute as the Battalion passes after attending the Plymouth Central Hall for the Centenary Civic Parade service.

Royal Review, 1983

As part of the 3,500 on parade these twelve young men were worthy representatives of the Plymouth Battalion at the Review of the B.B. by H.M. the Queen, our Patron at Holyrood House, Edinburgh, on the 2nd July. They are L/Cpl. Keith Glanfield and L/Cpl. Grant Bennett (4th Plymouth Company), Col/Sgt. David Wilcox and Cpl. Ivor Baker (5th Plymouth Company), Cpl. Simon Cox and Cpl. Christopher Warn (6th Plymouth Company), Sgt. Andrew Goodhead and Cpl. Andrew Williams (7th Plymouth Company), Sgt. Brian Earnshaw (8th Plymouth Company), Cpl. Andrew Milligan and Cpl. Neil Williams (9th Plymouth Company) and Cpl. Stephen Young (11th Plymouth Company).

The Battalion Executive Committee, 1983

The Lord Mayor of the City of Plymouth (Mr. Derek Mitchell), an honorary vice-president of the Battalion, pictured in the grounds of Pounds House with Graham Williams, (CS), Bill Lapthorn (VP), Richard Congdon (CS), Jim Stapleton (VP and Training Officer), Judith Pinch (JS), Malcolm Harrison (JS), Peter Bindschedler (President), Tom Babb (VP), Don Reeby (VP), Joyce Goodhead (Pre.JS), Michael Wilcox (Band Officer), Kenneth Banfield (Batt. Sec.) and Eric Chapman (ex District Field Officer).

CONCLUSION

We are now approaching the end of 1983 during which many events have been arranged to celebrate the centenary. The year was welcomed in by the Old Father Times beacon at Jennycliff arranged in conjunction with the English Tourist Board.

In February we had the Junior Section Missionary Rally, Company Sponsored Events Day, Battalion Band competition, Cross Country Run and Battalion Evening when officers and friends met together for a dinner.

March saw the Junior Section Choir Competition, Inter Uniformed Organisation Quiz, Junior Section Church Parade, Evening of Prayer and a very successful "house to house" collection and flag day. At the Family Fun Day in April a programme of games and competitions was enjoyed by officers, boys, parents and friends. In May we had the Civic Church Parade and Lord Mayor's Day. In the procession the Battalion Band occupied second position after the Royal Marines Band. Plymouth Hoe was the venue for the West of England District Band Contest in June.

A tea-table conference for chaplains, vice-presidents and captains was held in September. On Monday, 3rd October, a prayer meeting took place at St. Andrew's Church at 8 p.m., the hour when William Smith and the Hill brothers met in 1883 to seek God's blessing on their venture. On Tuesday, 4th October, the Battalion joined together for the centenary day celebration.

Two major events are outstanding to complete the year. *30th October:* Founder's Day Parade at Plymouth Central Hall when the Battalion will be joined by "old boys" and contingents from the Devon Division. *19th November:* Battalion Display in the Guildhall. The B.B. serves the church and through its work we pray that many boys and young men will commit themselves to Our Saviour Jesus Christ. There is a great deal being done and a great deal to be done.

*The Brigade makes a point of acknowledging God in everything, of putting Christ at the head of everything, and tries to do it in such a way that a boy will feel that the religious element in the work is a pleasure **and not a bore**.*

William A. Smith.

ARTS

ATHLETICS

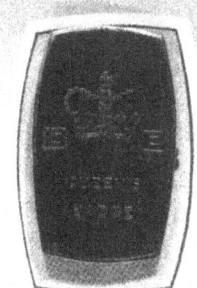
JUNIOR SECTION SERVICE

TARGET AWARDS

BANDSMAN'S

BUGLER'S

CRAFTS

CAMPING

CANOEING

CHRISTIAN EDUCATION

B.B. AWARDS
COMPANY SECTION

COMMUNICATIONS

    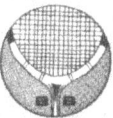

DRILL

DRUMMER'S

EXPEDITION

FIRST AID

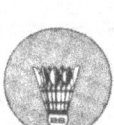

HOBBIES

LIFE SAVING

NATURALIST'S

Outline conditions
for all awards are printed
in the Handbook for Boys
1968 edition

THE DUKE OF EDINBURGH'S AWARD
ARM BADGE

Sportsman's Colours
are not worn in uniform
but on track suits, shorts, vests
or other informal wear

PHYSICAL RECREATION

PIPER'S

SAFETY   SAILING   SPORTSMAN'S   SWIMMING   SEAMANSHIP   COMPANY SECTION SERVICE

Arthur L. Clamp – the man behind the books

Arthur Leslie Clamp was a man of boundless energy with a passion for helping others, particularly through his love of history. A printer by trade, he started his career in a printing company before moving his family from Exeter to Plymouth to teach at the Plymouth College of Art and Design, where he eventually became the Head of the Printing Department.

A Devoted Family Man

Arthur with his five children.

Despite his love of teaching, Arthur prioritised his family, always making it home by 5:30pm for tea. He and his wife, Rosemary, raised five children: Susan, Angela, Elizabeth, David, and Steven. Arthur would often combine his love of family and history by taking his children on Sunday walks, encouraging them to appreciate historical monuments by taking photos or making crayon rubbings of gravestones for his books. The family home at 203 Elburton Road was a hub of activity, with a large garden, featuring a two-storey fort and a makeshift swimming pool.

A Lifelong Learner and Adventurer

Arthur's thirst for knowledge extended beyond history to a deep curiosity about the world. He was passionate about exploring different cultures, traditions, and cuisines, often taking advantage of his long summer holidays as a teacher to travel to places like India, Russia, South America, the middle east and the USA, sometimes bringing one of his children along. This adventurous spirit even influenced his home life, as seen by the short-lived family tradition of steam-cooking vegetables after a trip to Iceland.

History is a prominent feature of family days out

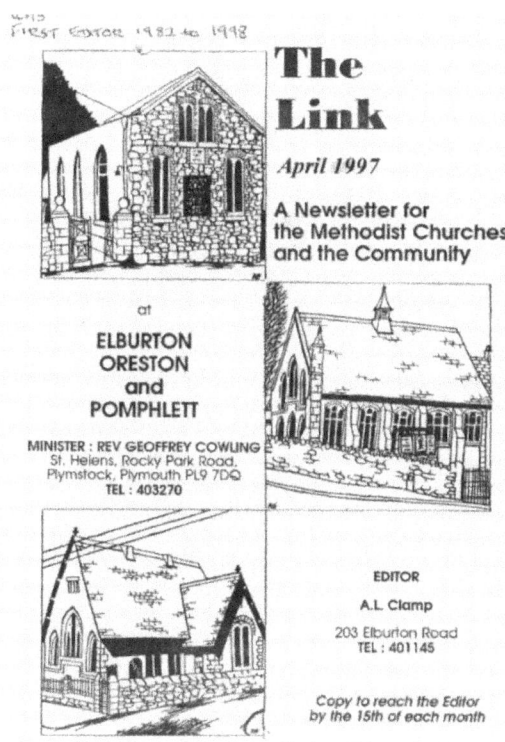

Community and Philanthropic Spirit

His commitment to serving others was evident in his long-standing involvement with the Elburton Methodist Church. He was the Sunday School Superintendent for over 15 years and served as the editor of the wider church's monthly newsletter, "The Link," for a similar duration. After Rosemary's very sad passing, Arthur later remarried and, following a chance encounter with a professor from India, established a connection with a missionary school in Chennai. Together with his new wife, Christine, he co-founded a "Sponsor a Child's Education" program that continues to this day.

Pictured left – The cover of 'The Link' complete with hand drawn sketches of each church by Angela
Below right – Arthur Clamp promoting his latest book
Below left – Arthur at home with his first wife, Rosemary
Below centre – Arthur on holiday with his second wife, Christine

A Legacy of Learning and Positivity

Arthur's greatest passion was history, which he brought to life through tireless research, documentation, and the many books he authored. He was driven by a need to "never be stuck in a rut," constantly seeking new experiences, meeting new people, and expanding his knowledge. With a positive attitude and a great sense of humour, he was always ready to help others, leaving a lasting impact on his family and community. His children, Susan, Angela, Elizabeth, David, and Steven, remember him with love and gratitude.

David Clamp, 2025

A Legacy of Local History

Below is the story of how Arthur L Clamp began writing books, in his own words, drafted shortly before he passed away in 2001. I have only made minor alterations to this text, correcting grammatical errors that he did not survive to correct himself. When I first discovered this text, I was shocked to see my name mentioned. It seems that, unbeknownst to me, I shared my first PC with him. I suspect he used it during the day when I was at school, although I do have one memory of sitting with him and showing him how it worked. It has been a pleasure to pick up where he left off and see his books republished and redistributed, and to know that I was part of the story, even back then. It was also fascinating to discover that his pricing structure matches the way I have tried to price the books, with a third going to local sellers and the rest covering printing costs with a little left over for my expenses.

I am his eldest grandson, and it is a privilege to curate his legacy, which we are calling 'The Clamp Collection'. The very last line of the text originally reads "The following pages list all the titles." Sadly, that page is missing and we have no record of all the books he published and knowing that some of those were researched by other authors makes the process of finding them even harder. I look forward to one day completing the collection and seeing them all available again. And maybe, one day, I'll even start writing my own to add to the series. For now, here is his story in his own words.

Steven Gibson, 2025

Writing and Publishing Booklets on Local Topics and Areas

I started this interest in either 1968 or 1969 when living in Woodford. I had by these dates established the Department of Printing and I think I must have been looking for something different to do. The first titles were of A5 size proofed from type set at Clarke, Doble and Brendon, Ltd., Plymouth printers, and then made up into pages and printed at Sawtell and Neilson, Ltd., Totnes.

Then began a slow process of getting them out to shops, etc. which proved to be more time consuming and difficult than actually researching, writing and getting the books into print. However, I persisted and opened a business account with Barclays Bank on the Broadway. I was advised to give it a title so I called it "Westway Publications". There came along another problem, one of storage of paper and finished books which was solved when the family moved to Elburton in 1970.

I changed the printer to Penwell, Ltd., Callington, Cornwall, as he was then just setting up himself and his prices seemed very reasonable. I did not get any of the printers to make up the complete books. I hand folded the flat printed sheets, stitched the books on a small manual table stitcher and trimmed them in a small hand turned guillotine which I bought from someone in Penzance for £40. It was brought up in a van.

The trouble and time going to and fro to Callington was too much so I transferred the printing to PDS Printers, Prince Rock, Plymouth, and I have been with them ever since. Now they are at Plympton which is easy to reach and they fold the flat sheets which was turning out to be a long chore which only saved a small part of the printing costs.

All my first titles were written by myself. I took the photographs and developed them in the loft of the house, the type was set by now on a computer situated in the house at Elburton from which I had collected photographic lengths of text to cut up and law down as pages.

At some point I decided that I would do my own film processing of lith film so I bought a large second hand process camera from Kingsbridge and learnt through trial and error to make line negatives of the text and halftone negatives of the illustrations which proved more difficult than I anticipated. The main problem was trying to keep the developer in the large dish at the correct temperature as any change would affect the developing time. I replaced this old camera with a brand new one bought from Croydon, Surrey, costing £900. This has turned out to be a great asset cutting out an expensive part of the printer's costs and one crucial aspect of the work which I could control.

By the middle 1970s there were many outlets I had contacted in Plymouth, up to Dartmoor, Exeter, around to Torbay, Totnes, Dartmouth and the South Hams. The market for local books was much greater than I had first thought and through getting to know many local people undertaking research themselves had the chance to help and make up books for other people who had in most instances, got together a collection of photographs with some text in a rather muddled way. Through my experience in print I was able to shape up their work and get it into print and in every case I had to pay the printer and let the person have the royalties. In the majority of titles produced in this manner this was another way of producing titles and it did give some profit to my work. However, I must say that in a few cases I lost out by either the other person getting the numbers wrong, not returning any monies from stock I delivered or they thought that more of their books should have been sold.

The print run was usually 1,000 copies and from time to time I have had reprints of 250 copies. It took about ten years to clear the first print run so I always had large stocks in the garage, workshop, etc. The numbers sold during the early years was about 7,000 copies a year increasing to around 9,000 copies and for the whole of the enterprise about 500,000 have been sold. The booklets have become part of the local scene and many people collect them, shops regularly order copies and I go around certain areas month by month restocking or replacing titles as necessary.

During the past year or so I have started setting the text on a Packard Bell PC, something which I should have done some years back. I share it with Steven Gibson, my grandson. There appears to be no end to the market for local books, but I could not earn a regular income because of the long time it takes to sell stock.

However, now exceeding 100 titles made up mainly of A4 twenty-four page booklets, some folded guides, with selling prices set with a third going to the shop which is the trade custom, the original idea has been quite successful and could go on for ever.

Apart from monetary benefits, however spasmodically these might be, I have learnt a lot myself, met many interesting people and have become part of the local scene with requests to give talks and to advise people about getting into print.

Arthur L Clamp, 2001

Death of local historical author

'He was an incredible character who was just loved by everybody who knew him'

A WELL-loved Elburton author has died at the age of 68.

Arthur Clamp (pictured right), who was one of the West Country's most successful writers, died at St Luke's Hospice, Turnchapel, after losing his battle against cancer.

Tributes have been flooding in for a man who was known in the community as a prominent writer and outgoing person.

He produced more than 140 titles during his life, dealing with both fiction, fact and history, often discussing West Country topics that were close to his heart.

One of his most acclaimed books was *The Plymouth Blitz*, and he also won credit for *The Rise and Fall of the Bearings of Membland Hall*, set in Noss Mayo.

He achieved sales of between 7,000 and 9,000 books every year and it is estimated that he has sold over half a million books, covering the areas of Plymouth, Dartmoor, Exeter, Torbay and the South Hams.

Mr Clamp was born in Mitcham, Surrey, in 1932, and was the eldest of four children.

He moved to Devon in 1941 to avoid the London air-raids.

Mr Clamp trained as a printer in Exeter and also gained a teachers' certificate in 1959 from Garnet College in London.

Plymouth College of Art, however, was to prove to be Mr Clamp's working home for the following 32 years until 1991, when he retired as head of the printing department.

He had a great interest in travel and had visited the USA, Tanzania, China, Russia, Peru, as well as travelling across Europe, where he presented talks and slide shows on his experiences as a writer.

Mr Clamp was a member of Elburton Methodist Church for many years, superintendent of the Sunday school and editor of the church newsletter, as well as being involved in much charity work.

He was president of the Plymouth and District Field Club and an active member of the Elburton Residents' Association.

He enjoyed leading walks on Dartmoor and historical tours throughout the West Country.

Mr Clamp married his first wife, Rosemary, in 1956 and they had five children – Susan, Angela, Elizabeth, David and Steven – and she died in 1987. He also had 11 grandchildren.

He leaves a wife Christine, after remarrying in 1991, and her two children and three grandchildren.

'He was an incredible character who was just loved by everybody who knew him,' said his wife.

'He will be missed by his family, his friends, the people he worked with and just everybody who knew him through his books.'

More than 300 mourners attended his funeral at Elburton Methodist Church on Monday.

'The attendance was a celebration of his life – he would have found that really special. It shows his vibrancy and love of people,' said Mrs Clamp.

Steven Clamp added that his father was 'a well respected and loved man, missed by a great many people throughout the South West and far beyond'.

This newspaper article, published by the Evening Herald on 17th August 2001, forms a good record of his life. Just as he encourages us to learn more about local history, we encourage you to learn a little about him. For that reason, we have included these pages at the back of all the most recently republished books, in honour of his memory and recognition of his contribution to the community.

www.ingramcontent.com/pod-product-compliance
Lightning Source LLC
Chambersburg PA
CBHW061402070526
44584CB00031B/4148